GARFIELD
Numero Uno

JIM DAVIS

RAVETTE PUBLISHING

First published by Ravette Publishing 2008.
Reprinted 2009

Printed and bound in Great Britain
for Ravette Publishing Limited,
PO Box 876, Horsham,
West Sussex RH12 9GH

ISBN: 978-1-84161-297-3

I'M GOING OUT IN SEARCH OF LOVE!
www.garfield.com
Distributed by Universal Press Syndicate

© 2004 PAWS INC All Rights Reserved

WE WILL NEVER SEE JON AGAIN
JIM DAVIS 8-20

Distributed by Universal Press Syndicate
www.garfield.com

STOP STARING AT ME!
© 2004 PAWS INC. All Rights Reserved

IT'S GOOD THAT WE HAVE THESE LITTLE DISCUSSIONS
JIM DAVIS 8-21

YOU'RE LATE!
www.garfield.com
Distributed by Universal Press Syndicate

BAT
© 2004 PAWS INC. All Rights Reserved

-AND YOUR FOLLOW-THROUGH NEEDS WORK!
NAG, NAG, NAG
JIM DAVIS 8-23

BAT
www.garfield.com
Distributed by Universal Press Syndicate

© 2004 PAWS INC. All Rights Reserved

"HELLO FROM THE FLOOR...
WISH YOU WERE HERE"
JIM DAVIS 8-24

HEY, GARFIELD
YO, YARN. WHAT'S UP?
www.garfield.com
Distributed by Universal Press Syndicate

NOT MUCH. JUST HANGING WITH MY COUSIN...
JIM DAVIS 8-25

HE'S A SPOOL OF THREAD
THERE IS A FAMILY RESEMBLANCE
© 2004 PAWS INC. All Rights Reserved.

JIM DAVIS 8-26
BINK
BINK BINK
Distributed by Universal Press Syndicate
www.garfield.com

BINK BINK
© 2004 PAWS INC All Rights Reserved

WHERE HAVE YOU...
IN THE HOT TUB, OKAY?!
BINK BINK

Distributed by Universal Press Syndicate

JIM DAVIS 8-27
www.garfield.com

YOU KNOW, EVEN BALLS OF YARN NEED CONDITIONER AFTER SHAMPOOING
I KNOW! I KNOW!
© 2004 PAWS, INC All Rights Reserved.

?
JIM DAVIS 8-28
www.garfield.com
Distributed by Universal Press Syndicate

SNIFF
SNIFF
SNIFF
© 2004 PAWS INC All Rights Reserved

?
DOGS DON'T
UNDERSTAND
BALLS OF YARN

SLEEP IN, OR EAT?...
SLEEP IN, OR EAT?
GARFIELD
www.garfield.com
Distributed by Universal Press Syndicate

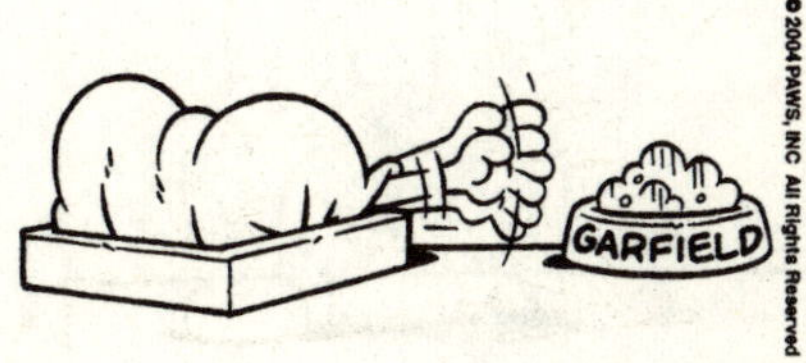

GARFIELD
© 2004 PAWS, INC All Rights Reserved

SLEEP IN
IT IS
GARFIELD
JIM DAVIS 8-30

ODIE

TOOOOOOOOO LATE
ODIE

AN ODE TO
DINNER...

BURRRRP!!!

BASED ON AN ACTUAL
EXPERIENCE
JIM DAVIS 1-6-9

WHEW!...IT SURE IS HOT

IT'S NOT SO MUCH THE HEAT, IT'S THE HUMIDITY

HE HAD THAT COMING
JIM DAVIS 9-2

I'VE GOTTA FIND A WAY TO COOL OFF
Distributed by Universal Press Syndicate
www.garfield.com

© 2004 PAWS, INC. All Rights Reserved.

ARE THOSE FROZEN PEAS?!
THEY'RE ALL THE RAGE THIS SEASON
JIM DAVIS 9-3

I'VE DISCOVERED A NEW WAY TO BEAT THE SUMMER HEAT
www.garfield.com
Distributed by Universal Press Syndicate

© 2004 PAWS INC. All Rights Reserved

TURN UP THE AIR CONDITIONING!
WHOP!
POO!
JIM DAVIS 9-4

www.garfield.com
Distributed by Universal Press Syndicate

Z
GO
CAT AT WORK
© 2004 PAWS INC. All Rights Reserved

THE FLAG MOUSE WAS ACTUALLY A NICE TOUCH
JIM DAVIS 9-6

GOOD WORK, GARFIELD! BE EVER VIGILANT!
JIM DAVIS 9-7
Distributed by Universal Press Syndicate

HEY! HEY! HEY!
www.garfield.com
© 2004 PAWS INC All Rights Reserved

DON'T TURN THE PAGE YET!
IF YOU'RE GOING TO READ OVER MY SHOULDER, READ FASTER!

JiM DAViS 9-8
www.garfield.com
Distributed by Universal Press Syndicate

© 2004 PAWS INC All Rights Reserved

WOULDN'T YOU HAVE A BETTER CHANCE OF CATCHING THE MOUSE IF YOU ACTUALLY CHASED HIM?
I'M COUNTING ON HIS PULLING UP LAME

EEK! A MOUSE!
JIM DAVIS 9-9
www.garfield.com
Distributed by Universal Press Syndicate

© 2004 PAWS INC. All Rights Reserved

COME ON. IT'S HIS BIRTHDAY

I'M TIRED
www.garfield.com
Distributed by Universal Press Syndicate

THEN HAVE
A SEAT
© 2004 PAWS INC. All Rights Reserved

PERHAPS I'VE BEEN
TOO LAX ON THIS
CAT-MOUSE THING
JIM DAVIS 9-10

GARFIELD! CATCH THE MOUSE!
I WILL
www.garfield.com
Distributed by Universal Press Syndicate

BUT, BECAUSE I'M SUCH A GREAT SPORT, I'M GIVING HIM A HEAD START
© 2004 PAWS INC. All Rights Reserved.

ABOUT A TWO-WEEK HEAD START
JIM DAVIS 9-11

TIME TO EXPLORE THE OUTER REACHES OF MY UNIVERSE
Distributed by Universal Press Syndicate
www.garfield.com

© 2004 PAWS INC All Rights Reserved

JIM DAVIS 9-13

GRRR
ODIE HAS SOMETHING CORNERED
www.garfield.com
Distributed by Universal Press Syndicate

GRRR
© 2004 PAWS INC All Rights Reserved

IT'S THE CORNER
GRRR
JIM DAVIS 9-14

THERE'S SURELY SOMETHING ON WORTH WATCHING
CLICK
CLICK
CLICK
www.garfield.com
Distributed by Universal Press Syndicate

CLICK
CLICK
CLICK
CLICK
CLICK
JIM DAVIS 9-15
© 2004 PAWS INC All Rights Reserved

IT'S THE ALL-LASAGNA CHANNEL!
THE MOTHER LODE!

www.garfield.com
Distributed by Universal Press Syndicate

© 2004 PAWS INC All Rights Reserved

JIM DAVIS 9-16

IT WAS SO STRANGE...MY DATE POSSESSED THE ABILITY TO BECOME INVISIBLE!
Distributed by Universal Press Syndicate
www.garfield.com

UH, JON...
ONE MINUTE SHE WAS THERE AND, THE NEXT MINUTE...
© 2004 PAWS INC All Rights Reserved

SHE DITCHED YOU
POOF
JIM DAVIS 9-17

I WONDER IF THEY'LL MAKE A MOVIE ABOUT MY LIFE SOMEDAY
www.garfield.com
Distributed by Universal Press Syndicate

ABSOLUTELY!
© 2004 PAWS INC All Rights Reserved

BUT MORE LIKE A SOCK PUPPET SHOW
JIM DAVIS 9-18

NAP TIME
www.garfield.com
Distributed by Universal Press Syndicate

THUD
JIM DAVIS 9-20
© 2004 PAWS INC All Rights Reserved

YOU'RE PATHETIC
Z

AHHHHHHHH
Distributed by Universal Press Syndicate   www.garfield.com

THE NAP...
© 2004 PAWS INC All Rights Reserved

BEDTIME'S APPETIZER
JIM DAVIS 9-21

SHOES

SHOES

BUNK
BEDS
SHOES
JiM DAViS 9-22

Z

NAPS ARE ALWAYS
MORE FUN WHEN
THEY'RE SNUCK
JIM DAVIS 9-23

Z
Distributed by Universal Press Syndicate
www.garfield.com

Z
CLICK
© 2004 PAWS INC All Rights Reserved

Z
JiM DAViS 9-24

WHAT IF I WERE TO JUST LIE HERE FOREVER...
JIM DAVIS 9-25

AND NEVER GET UP AGAIN?

WHAT ARE YOU DOING?
THINKING HAPPY THOUGHTS

BURP

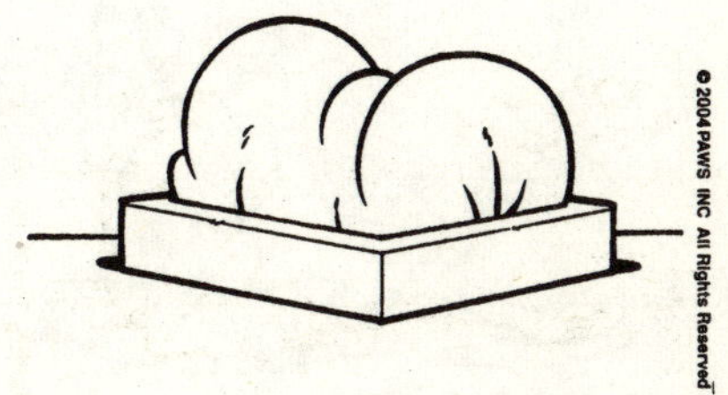

GASP!!!
JIM DAVIS 9-27

Distributed by Universal Press Syndicate
www.garfield.com

HAVE A COUPON FOR A FREE CHEESEBURGER!
OKAY!
© 2004 PAWS INC All Rights Reserved

HEY! THIS HAS EXPIRED!
JIM DAVIS 9-28

LOOK, GARFIELD!
www.garfield.com
Distributed by Universal Press Syndicate

SCARY, HUH?
SCARY? YOU'RE JUST WEARING A GROCERY SACK!
© 2004 PAWS INC. All Rights Reserved.

I'M AN EMPTY GROCERY SACK!
EMPTY?!
JIM DAVIS 9-29

I'VE BEEN LYING HERE FOR 83 HOURS AND 17 MINUTES WITHOUT MOVING A MUSCLE
www.garfield.com
Distributed by Universal Press Syndicate

YES! ONLY 10 SECONDS AWAY FROM MY PERSONAL BES...
© 2004 PAWS INC All Rights Reserved

NUTS
JIM DAVIS 9-30

ELLEN, WHEN YOU SAY HURTFUL THINGS TO ME, I JUST WANT TO CURL UP AND WITHER AWAY
www.garfield.com
Distributed by Universal Press Syndicate

JIM DAViS 10-1
© 2004 PAWS INC All Rights Reserved

SHE'S SAYING HURTFUL THINGS
SO WITHER ALREADY

TODAY IS A TEENSE LESS BORING THAN YESTERDAY
www.garfield.com
Distributed by Universal Press Syndicate

JiM DAViS 10-2

PARTY ON
© 2004 PAWS, INC. All Rights Reserved

GARFIELD! DID YOU EAT ALL THREE OF THOSE CAKES I BAKED?!
JIM DAVIS 10-4

NOPE

TWO AND A HALF

GARFIELD...
JIM DAVIS 10-5

YOU'VE BEEN EATING IN BED AGAIN, HAVEN'T YOU?

SO, SHERLOCK, WHAT TIPPED YOU OFF?

RIIING!
HELLO?
Distributed by Universal Press Syndicate   www.garfield.com

NO, NO...
IT'S
ALL RIGHT
© 2004 PAWS INC All Rights Reserved

THAT WAS
THE TITANIC.
THEY SPOTTED
AN ORANGE
ICEBERG
I WONDER
IF YOU
FLOAT?
JIM DAVIS 10-6

I NOW DO WEIGHT AND FORTUNES
YOU'RE ON
Distributed by Universal Press Syndicate
www.garfield.com

YOU'RE FAT
...AND MY FORTUNE?
© 2004 PAWS INC All Rights Reserved

I PREDICT YOU'RE GOING TO STOMP ME FLAT
YOU'RE GOOD
JIM DAVIS 10-7

IF YOU CONTINUE TO GAIN WEIGHT AT YOUR CURRENT RATE...
www.garfield.com
Distributed by Universal Press Syndicate

IN 17 YEARS, YOU'LL BLOT OUT THE SUN!
JIM DAVIS 10-8
© 2004 PAWS INC. All Rights Reserved

WHERE ARE YOU GOING?
TO GET A DONUT AND A FLASHLIGHT

LOW-FAT
CAT FOOD
JiM DAViS 10-9
www.garfield.com
Distributed by Universal Press Syndicate
LOW FAT
CAT FOOD
GARFIELD

GARFIELD
© 2004 PAWS INC All Rights Reserved

DO I LOOK LIKE A
LOW-FAT CAT?!
GARFIELD

IF YOU CLOSE YOUR EYES, YOU CAN PRETEND THIS LETTUCE IS CHOCOLATE CAKE
www.garfield.com
Distributed by Universal Press Syndicate

JIM DAVIS 10-11
© 2004 PAWS INC All Rights Reserved

IF YOU CLOSE YOUR EYES, I CAN HAVE REAL CHOCOLATE CAKE!

HEY, JON, CHECK OUT MY NEW DIET!
www.garfield.com
Distributed by Universal Press Syndicate

MUNCH MUNCH
GULP
© 2004 PAWS INC All Rights Reserved

DID YOU NOTICE I CHEWED BEFORE I SWALLOWED?
JIM DAVIS 10-12

HOW'S THE DIET GOING?
HEY!
JIM DAVIS 10-13
www.garfield.com
Distributed by Universal Press Syndicate

SOMEBODY OUT THERE'S EATING!
© 2004 PAWS INC All Rights Reserved

I WITHDRAW THE QUESTION
BACON!

HOW'S THE DIET GOING?
GREAT!
Distributed by Universal Press Syndicate
www.garfield.com

I'VE CUT OUT SNACKS
© 2004 PAWS INC All Rights Reserved

I DID, HOWEVER, HAVE ELEVEN LUNCHES
JIM DAVIS 10-14

I'VE EATEN ALL THE DONUTS...
Distributed by Universal Press Syndicate
www.garfield.com

NOW THEY CAN'T TEMPT ME TO CHEAT ON MY DIET
© 2004 PAWS INC All Rights Reserved

FLAWLESS LOGIC, IF EVER I'VE HEARD IT!
JIM DAVIS 10-15

ARE YOU HAVING A GOOD TIME?
JIM DAVIS 10-16
© 2004 PAWS INC All Rights Reserved.

BECAUSE I'M NOT!
SPLOT
www.garfield.com
Distributed by Universal Press Syndicate

WAIT. THAT WAS KIND OF FUN

WHY ARE CATS SO MYSTERIOUS?
JIM DAVIS 10-18
www.garfield.com
Distributed by Universal Press Syndicate

ALLOW ME TO EXPLAIN BY WAY OF AN INTERPRETIVE DANCE
© 2004 PAWS INC All Rights Reserved

WHY IS A DOG'S NOSE SO COLD?
JIM DAVIS 10-19
www.garfield.com
Distributed by Universal Press Syndicate

LET'S FIND OUT
© 2004 PAWS INC. All Rights Reserved

AH-HA...

JIM DAVIS 10-20
www.garfield.com
Distributed by Universal Press Syndicate

GONG
© 2004 PAWS INC. All Rights Reserved

WHERE DID YOU GET THE GONG?
SPANKY'S HOUSE OF ALL THINGS DINNER
GARFIELD

CATS ARE VERY CLEAN ANIMALS
www.garfield.com
Distributed by Universal Press Syndicate

THEY CLEAN THEMSELVES WITH THEIR TONGUES
© 2004 PAWS INC All Rights Reserved

BUT NOT YOU!
WE'RE OUT OF CONDITIONER
JIM DAVIS 10-21

GARFIELD, I THINK THAT GIRL DOWN THE COUNTER IS LOOKING AT ME!
NO SHE ISN'T

I THINK SHE WANTS TO MEET ME!
NO SHE DOESN'T
JIM DAVIS 10-22

I MAY HAVE BEEN MISTAKEN
YES, YOU WERE

I'M SO BORED I CAN'T BELIEVE IT
Distributed by Universal Press Syndicate
www.garfield.com

NOT ME
© 2004 PAWS INC All Rights Reserved

I CAN BELIEVE IT
JIM DAVIS 10-23

WOW!
JIM DAVIS 10-25
Distributed by Universal Press Syndicate
www.garfield.com

LOOK AT
THAT
BIG, FAT,
ORANGE-
© 2004 PAWS INC. All Rights Reserved

PUMPKIN

Distributed by Universal Press Syndicate
www.garfield.com

HMMM, JUST LIKE ODIE...
JIM DAVIS 10 26

THE LIGHT'S ON, BUT NOBODY'S HOME
© 2004 PAWS, INC All Rights Reserved

...THAT MONSTER COULD BE ANYWHERE!
www.garfield.com
Distributed by Universal Press Syndicate

...HE COULD EVEN BE RIGHT BEHIND—
JIM DAVIS 10-27
© 2004 PAWS INC All Rights Reserved

HI, GUYS...
CUE THE BLOODCURDLING SCREAMS

LARRY, DON'T!
...DON'T GO
IN THERE!

I MUST GO
IN THERE,
MARGARET!
BRAVE,
LARRY

AAAAGGGHHH!
BRAVE,
STUPID,
LARRY

TONIGHT WE'RE SPEAKING WITH A BIG, FAT, CREEPY MONSTER
GLAD TO BE HERE
www.garfield.com
Distributed by Universal Press Syndicate

SO, WHERE DO YOU LIVE?
UNDER YOUR BED
JIM DAVYS 10-29

UHHHH...
AND AREN'T YOU A LITTLE OLD TO BE WEARING BUNNY SLIPPERS?
SWEET DREAMS
© 2004 PAWS INC All Rights Reserved

WE'RE SPEAKING TODAY WITH AN ACTUAL VAMPIRE
www.garfield.com
Distributed by Universal Press Syndicate

GOOD MORNING, SIR
THANK YO- ...MORNING?
JiM DAViS 10-30

MORNING?!!
THEY JUST MIGHT WANT TO DRAW THOSE BLINDS
© 2004 PAWS INC All Rights Reserved

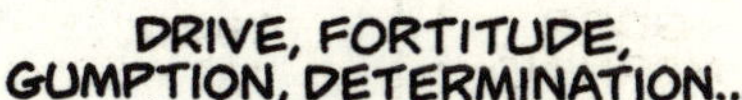

JIM DAVIS 11-1

TIME TO TAKE
A BREAK, ODIE
Distributed by Universal Press Syndicate   www.garfield.com

© 2004 PAWS INC. All Rights Reserved

OUR BREAKS ARE SO LONG,
OUR BREAKS NEED BREAKS
JIM DAVIS 11-2

AH...
AH...

CHOO!

SO, WOULD YOU LIKE SOME TOAST?
NOT IN THIS LIFETIME
JIM DAVIS 11-3

SOMETIMES I SLEEP SO MUCH I CAN'T TELL IF IT'S DAY OR NIGHT

SOMETIMES I EAT SO MUCH I CAN'T TELL IF I'M HUNGRY OR FULL

IGNORANCE IS BLISS
JIM DAVIS 11-4

OH, ELLEN...
JiM DAViS 11-5
www.garfield.com
Distributed by Universal Press Syndicate

MY LOVE FOR YOU IS LIKE AN ENDLESS VOID...
© 2004 PAWS INC. All Rights Reserved

WAIT! WRONG SIMILE!
THAT'S THE ONE ABOUT YOUR HEAD

Distributed by Universal Press Syndicate
www.garfield.com

SACK
TIME

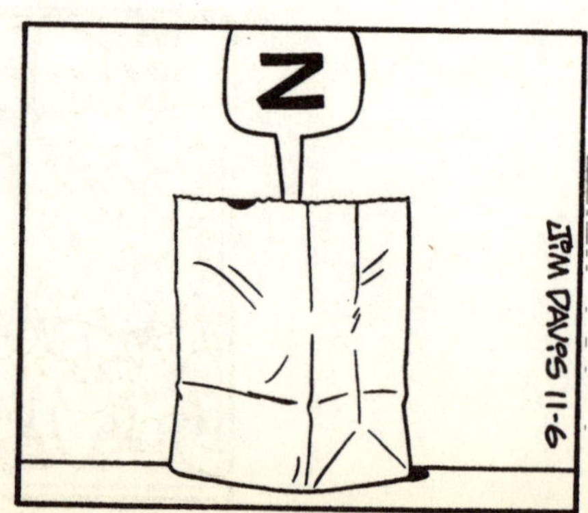

Z
JiM DAViS 11-6

THERE ARE THINGS IN LIFE WE JUST HAVE TO ADMIT WE CAN'T CONTROL
Distributed by Universal Press Syndicate
www.garfield.com

JPM DAVPS 11-8
© 2004 PAWS INC. All Rights Reserved

LIKE YOU
YEAH, I'M A REAL FORCE OF NATURE

HEY, I KNOW I'M FAT...
SO WHAT?
Distributed by Universal Press Syndicate   www.garfield.com

I'M FAT, AND
I'M BEAUTIFUL!
© 2004 PAWS, INC. All Rights Reserved

NARCISSISM...USE IT
OR LOSE IT
JIM DAVIS 11-9

SAY, GOOD LOOKIN'
Distributed by Universal Press Syndicate
www.garfield.com

YOU LOOK FABULOUS!
© 2004 PAWS INC. All Rights Reserved

HEY, MIRRORS NEED LOVE, TOO
JiM DAViS 11-10

OH,
GEEZ
www.garfield.com
Distributed by Universal Press Syndicate

I NEED A
HAIRCUT BAD
© 2004 PAWS, INC All Rights Reserved

TRY SHEDDING,
IT'S CHEAPER!
JIM DAVIS 11-11

I THOUGHT I WAS GOING TO SEIZE THE DAY...
www.garfield.com
Distributed by Universal Press Syndicate

BUT THE DAY SEIZED ME INSTEAD
POOR JON
© 2004 PAWS INC. All Rights Reserved

LIFE'S A SALAD BAR, AND HE JUST KEEPS SMACKING HIS FOREHEAD ON THE SNEEZE GUARD
JIM DAVIS 11-12

www.garfield.com
Distributed by Universal Press Syndicate

© 2004 PAWS INC. All Rights Reserved

SO, HOW WAS YOUR DAY?
BETTER THAN YOURS
JIM DAVIS 11-13

OPERATORS ARE STANDING BY TO TAKE YOUR ORDER!

I WON'T BE ORDERING ANYTHING...YOU MAY TAKE THE REST OF THE NIGHT OFF
HELLO? HELLO?
JIM DAVIS 11-15

AND NOW, BACK TO OUR NATURE SPECIAL...
Distributed by Universal Press Syndicate
www.garfield.com

SHARKS WHO LOVE TOES
JIM DAVIS 11-16

© 2004 PAWS INC All Rights Reserved

WE HAVE A
GREAT SHOW!
www.garfield.com
Distributed by Universal Press Syndicate

AND WE KNOW
YOU'LL ENJOY IT!
JIM DAVIS 11-17
© 2004 PAWS INC All Rights Reserved

NOBODY TELLS
ME WHAT
TO DO
CLICK

WELCOME BACK TO "TELEPATHIC JOKES"!

ALREADY HEARD IT
CLICK

I LOVE HOSTING
THIS SHOW
www.garfield.com
Distributed by Universal Press Syndicate

-ABSOLUTELY
LOVE IT!
© 2004 PAWS INC. All Rights Reserved

IT MEANS I
DON'T HAVE
TO WATCH
IT
I WISH
I
HOSTED IT
JIM DAVIS 11-19

OH, LANCE, THE BOMB IS ABOUT TO GO OFF!
Distributed by Universal Press Syndicate
www.garfield.com

DON'T WORRY, MARION. HERE COMES SUPER DOG TO SAVE US!
© 2004 PAWS INC All Rights Reserved
JIM DAVIS 11-20

BARK! BARK! BARK!
WHERE IS HE GOING?!
SPOTTED A SQUIRREL

GARFIELD, ARE YOU HAPPY?
GARFIELD

GARFIELD

NO FOOD, NO HAPPY
JIM DAVIS 11-22
GARFIELD

COME ON OUT!
NO!
JIM DAVIS 11-23
Distributed by Universal Press Syndicate
www.garfield.com

COME AND GET ME, BOZO!
© 2004 PAWS INC All Rights Reserved

DINNER, GARFIELD?
NO THANKS. I JUST ATE A SMALL HOUSE
GARFIELD

Distributed by Universal Press Syndicate
www.garfield.com

© 2004 PAWS INC All Rights Reserved

THAT WAS A NUTRITIOUS MEAL!
YEAH, I DIDN'T LIKE IT EITHER
JIM DAVIS 11-24

THERE YOU ARE!
JIM DAVIS 11-26
Distributed by Universal Press Syndicate
www.garfield.com

I LOVE LASAGNA!
© 2004 PAWS INC All Rights Reserved

BUT ALAS, IT WAS ONLY A FLING

GARFIELD,
GARFIELD,
GARFIELD

JUST LOOK
AT YOU...

HE'S RIGHT... I
DO LOOK HUNGRY
JiM DAViS 11-27

CHRISTMAS IS COMING, AND YOU KNOW WHAT THAT MEANS...

THAT'S EXACTLY WHAT THAT MEANS
JIM DAVIS 11-29

HEY, YOU!
www.garfield.com
Distributed by Universal Press Syndicate

THAT'S MORE LIKE IT
© 2004 PAWS INC. All Rights Reserved
JIM DAVIS 11-30

CHRISTMAS IS COMING...
GET WITH THE PROGRAM!
DECEMBER

CALENDARS...THEY HURRY
ALL YEAR LONG
DEC.
JIM DAVIS 12-1
www.garfield.com

-UNTIL
DECEMBER...
DEC.
Distributed by Universal Press Syndicate
© 2004 PAWS INC All Rights Reserved

THEN THEY
MOSEY!
DEC.

YOU KNOW, THEY SAY CHRISTMAS COOKIE CALORIES DON'T COUNT
www.garfield.com
Distributed by Universal Press Syndicate

I BELIEVE THAT
© 2004 PAWS INC. All Rights Reserved.

NOW, TO CONVINCE MY BELLY
JIM DAVIS 12-2

SANTA CLAUS KNOWS IF YOU'RE GOOD OR BAD
www.garfield.com
Distributed by Universal Press Syndicate

THAT'S COOL
© 2004 PAWS INC All Rights Reserved

BUT DOES HE KNOW I'M DANGEROUS?
JIM DAVIS 12-3

SNIFF
SNIFF
JIM DAViS 12-4
Distributed by Universal Press Syndicate
www.garfield.com

IT SMELLS
LIKE
CHRISTMAS!
© 2004 PAWS, INC. All Rights Reserved

IT MUST BE THAT
TIME OF YEAR...
HINT
HINT

HEY! NICE HAT!
www.garfield.com
Distributed by Universal Press Syndicate

THAT'S THE OL'
CHRISTMAS SPIRIT!
© 2004 PAWS, INC All Rights Reserved

HE MUST HAVE
BEEN TALKING ABOUT
MY CHRISTMAS
COOKIE STORAGE
DEVICE
JIM DAVIS 12-6

I LOVE THIS TIME OF YEAR
Distributed by Universal Press Syndicate
www.garfield.com
JIM DAVIS 12-7

COOKIES...PRESENTS...
COOKIES...FAMILY...
COOKIES...
© 2004 PAWS INC All Rights Reserved

MORE COOKIES...
WHO ATE ALL THE COOKIES?!

ALL RIGHT, I'LL TAKE YOU TO SEE SANTA IF YOU PROMISE TO BEHAVE
www.garfield.com
Distributed by Universal Press Syndicate

© 2004 PAWS INC All Rights Reserved

WE'RE NOT GOING
C'MON! THAT WAS MY BEST FAKE SINCERE SMILE!
JIM DAVIS 12-8

Dear Santa,

I have been very good all year... And...

BOY... FICTION IS HARD
JIM DAVIS 12-9

SO, GARFIELD, IS SANTA GOING TO BRING YOU LOTS OF PRESENTS THIS YEAR?
JIM DAVIS 12-10
www.garfield.com

HE'D BETTER!
© 2004 PAWS INC. All Rights Reserved

WE HAVE A CONTRACT AND I HAVE A GOOD LAWYER
Distributed by Universal Press Syndicate

WE RETURN NOW TO
"THE LITTLEST ELF"

JIM DAVIS 12-11

HEY, A CHRISTMAS CARD
www.garfield.com
Distributed by Universal Press Syndicate

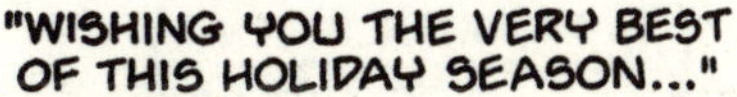

"WISHING YOU THE VERY BEST OF THIS HOLIDAY SEASON..."

© 2004 PAWS, INC. All Rights Reserved.

-"AND STOP CALLING ME AND ASKING ME OUT, YOU DORK. ELLEN"
WARM, SINCERE, AND IT GETS THE JOB DONE
JiM DAViS 12-13

LOOK, GARFIELD, ANOTHER CHRISTMAS CARD!
Distributed by Universal Press Syndicate
www.garfield.com

I WONDER IF IT'S FROM DOC BOY?
© 2004 PAWS, INC All Rights Reserved

DOES THE POSTMARK HAVE A COW ON IT?
THE POSTMARK HAS A COW ON IT
JIM DAVIS 12-14

WE NOW RETURN TO "HAROLD FENSTERNICK..."
© 2004 PAWS, INC All Rights Reserved
JIM DAVIS 12-15

"-THE REGULAR GUY WHO SAVED CHRISTMAS"
www.garfield.com
Distributed by Universal Press Syndicate

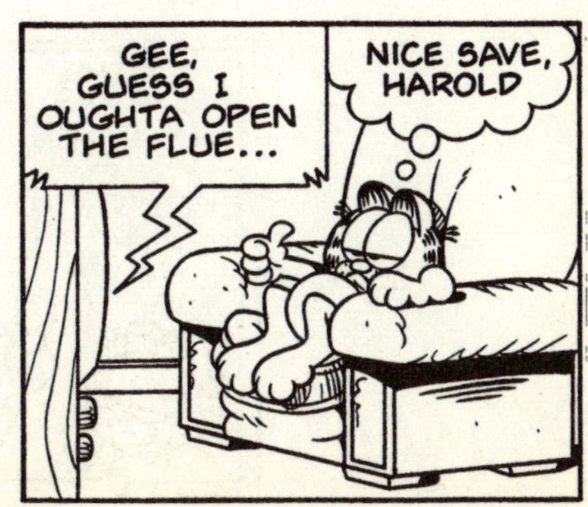

GEE, GUESS I OUGHTA OPEN THE FLUE...
NICE SAVE, HAROLD

A BOX!
JIM DAVIS 12-16

NO, WAIT! NOT AT THIS TIME OF YEAR... IT'S NOT A BOX...
www.garfield.com
© 2004 PAWS, INC. All Rights Reserved.

IT'S A NAKED CHRISTMAS PRESENT!
Distributed by Universal Press Syndicate

I'M WRAPPING CHRISTMAS PRESENTS NOW...
JIM DAViS 12-17
www.garfield.com
Distributed by Universal Press Syndicate

SO DON'T COME IN HERE!
© 2004 PAWS, INC. All Rights Reserved

-AND NO VIDEO SURVEILLANCE CAMERAS!
TOO LATE

WE NOW RETURN TO "STEWART, THE CHRISTMAS LEECH"
© 2004 PAWS, INC. All Rights Reserved
www.garfield.com
Distributed by Universal Press Syndicate

GATHER 'ROUND, ELVES! HO! HO! H-...HUH?
JIM DAVIS 12-18

GAAHHH! GET IT OFF ME!! GET IT OFF!!!
WOW. STEW'S THIRSTY

HEY, CAT
HEY, SPIDER

I HAVE A GIFT FOR YOU... LOWER AWAY, GUYS!

HAVE A LICK
OVER MY DEAD TONGUE
JIM DAVIS 12-20

THE CHRISTMAS TREE SEEMS TO BE MISSING SOMETHING...
JIM DAVIS 12-21

GOT IT!
© 2004 PAWS, INC. All Rights Reserved
www.garfield.com
Distributed by Universal Press Syndicate

IT NEEDS MORE PRESENTS!

JIM DAVIS 12-22
Distributed by Universal Press Syndicate
www.garfield.com

GARFIELD, GO BACK TO BED
I CAN'T
© 2004 PAWS, INC All Rights Reserved

WHO GIVES PRESENTS TO SANTA?

CHRISTMAS IS ONLY TWO DAYS AWAY!
Distributed by Universal Press Syndicate
www.garfield.com

172,800 SECONDS!
© 2004 PAWS, INC. All Rights Reserved.

YOU LOOK PREOCCUPIED
172,797 SECONDS...
JIM DAVIS 12-23

CHRISTMAS
EVE...

SLEEP IS NOT
AN OPTION
JIM DAVIS 12-24

IT'S CHRISTMAS AGAIN, OLD FRIEND...
Distributed by Universal Press Syndicate
www.garfield.com

TIME FOR US TO EXCHANGE OUR ANNUAL CHRISTMAS GIFT...
© 2004 PAWS, INC. All Rights Reserved.

MERRY CHRISTMAS!
JIM DAVIS

THAT WAS A GREAT CHRISTMAS, WASN'T IT?
YEAH...
Distributed by Universal Press Syndicate
www.garfield.com

REMEMBER THAT NUT LOG GRANDMA SENT US?
OH, YEAH...

YOU SHOULD...YOU ATE THE WHOLE THING
I'LL BE DIGESTING THAT BABY TILL THE SPRING THAW
© 2004 PAWS, INC All Rights Reserved
JIM DAVIS 12-27

HELLO, LISA? IT'S JON ARBUCKLE...
© 2004 PAWS, INC All Rights Reserved
Distributed by Universal Press Syndicate   www.garfield.com

-AND THERE JUST HAPPENS TO BE A HUGE HOLE IN MY SOCIAL CALENDAR FOR NEW YEAR'S EVE
JiM DAViS 12-28

SHE TOLD ME TO TAKE MY CALENDAR AND SPACKLE IT
HOW DIPLOMATIC

DENISE, IT'S JON...

HEY, HOWZABOUT JUST THE TWO OF US GOING OUT ON NEW YEAR'S EVE?
JIM DAVIS 12-29

GUESS IT'LL JUST BE THE ONE OF US
ARE YOU SURE YOU WANT TO GO OUT WITH YOU?

ELLEN, WILL YOU GO OUT WITH ME ON NEW YEAR'S EVE?
Distributed by Universal Press Syndicate
www.garfield.com

WHAT'S THAT SOUND?... SODA, YOU SAY?
JPM DAVPS 12-30

OUT YOUR NOSE, YOU SAY?
SO FAR, AND YET SO FAR
© 2004 PAWS, INC All Rights Reserved.

NEW YEAR'S EVE...
Distributed by Universal Press Syndicate
www.garfield.com

AND HE'S ALL DRESSED UP WITH NO PLACE TO GO
© 2004 PAWS, INC All Rights Reserved

WHAT A PERFECTLY GOOD WASTE OF A PERFECTLY BAD SUIT
JIM DAVIS 12-31

HONNNK!!!

YOU DO THAT TO ME EVERY YEAR!
BUT WHAT BETTER WAY TO START THE YEAR

—THAN WITH A CRUEL LAUGH AT YOUR EXPENSE?
www.garfield.com
Distributed by Universal Press Syndicate

WELL, THE HOLIDAYS ARE OFFICIALLY OVER
JIM DAVIS 1-3
www.garfield.com
Distributed by Universal Press Syndicate

TIME TO GET BACK TO MY OLD ROUTINE...
©2005 PAWS, INC All Rights Reserved.

WHAT ARE YOU DOING?
MY OLD ROUTINE

I THINK I'LL
LIE HERE
ALL DAY
www.garfield.com
Distributed by Universal Press Syndicate

I CAN'T THINK OF ANYTHING
TO DO TODAY
© 2005 PAWS, INC. All Rights Reserved

BUM
JIM DAVIS 1-4

GARFIELD, ALL YOU
DO IS SLEEP
JIM DAVIS 1-5
www.garfield.com
Distributed by Universal Press Syndicate

SLEEP, AND SLEEP, AND
SLEEP, AND SLEEP
© 2005 PAWS, INC. All Rights Reserved

KNOW WHAT I CALL
SOMEONE LIKE THAT?
FRISKY?

TIME FOR A NICE NAP...
THE ICE-CREAM TRUCK IS COMING UP THE STREET!
JIM DAVIS 1-6
©2005 PAWS, INC. All Rights Reserved

www.garfield.com
Distributed by Universal Press Syndicate

LOOKS LIKE WE'VE GOT OURSELVES A REAL DILEMMA HERE...

OTHER GARFIELD BOOKS AVAILABLE

Pocket Books	Price	ISBN
Am I Bothered?	£3.99	978-1-84161-286-7
Compute This!	£3.50	978-1-84161-194-5
Don't Ask!	£3.99	978-1-84161-247-8
Feed Me!	£3.99	978-1-84161-242-3
Get Serious	£3.99	978-1-84161-265-2
Gooooooal	£3.99	978-1-84161-329-1
Gotcha!	£3.50	978-1-84161-226-3
I Am What I Am!	£3.99	978-1-84161-243-0
I Don't Do Perky	£3.99	978-1-84161-195-2
Kowabunga	£3.99	978-1-84161-246-1
Pop Star	£3.50	978-1-84161-151-8
S.W.A.L.K.	£3.50	978-1-84161-225-6
Talk to the Paw (new)	£3.99	978-1-84161-317-8
Time to Delegate	£3.99	978-1-84161-206-6
Wan2tlk?	£3.99	978-1-84161-264-5
What's Not to Like?	£3.99	978-1-84161-285-0

Theme Books	Price	ISBN
Creatures Great & Small	£3.99	978-1-85304-998-9
Entertains You	£4.50	978-1-84161-221-8
Pigging Out	£4.50	978-1-85304-893-7
Slam Dunk!	£4.50	978-1-84161-222-5
The Seasons	£3.99	978-1-85304-999-6

2-in-1 Theme Books	Price	ISBN
All In Good Taste	£6.99	978-1-84161-209 6
Easy Does It	£6.99	978-1-84161-191 4
Lazy Daze	£6.99	978-1-84161-208 9
Licensed to Thrill	£6.99	978-1-84161-192 1
Out For The Couch	£6.99	978-1-84161-144 0
The Gruesome Twosome	£6.99	978-1-84161-143 3

Classics	Price	ISBN
Volume One	£6.99	978-1-85304-970-5
Volume Two	£7.99	978-1-85304-971-2
Volume Three	£7.99	978-1-85304-996-5
Volume Four	£6.99	978-1-85304-997-2
Volume Five	£6.99	978-1-84161-022-1
Volume Six	£7.99	978-1-84161-023-8
Volume Seven	£5.99	978-1-84161-088-7
Volume Eight	£7.99	978-1-84161-089-4
Volume Nine	£6.99	978-1-84161-149-5
Volume Ten	£6.99	978-1-84161-150-1
Volume Eleven	£7.99	978-1-84161-175-4
Volume Twelve	£7.99	978-1-84161-176-1
Volume Thirteen	£6.99	978-1-84161-206-5

Classics (cont'd ...)	**Price**	**ISBN**
Volume Fourteen	£6.99	978-1-84161-207-2
Volume Fifteen	£5.99	978-1-84161-232-4
Volume Sixteen	£5.99	978-1-84161-233-1
Volume Seventeen	£7.99	978-1-84161-250-8
Volume Eighteen	£6.99	978-1-84161 251-5
Volume Nineteen	£6.99	978-1-84161-303-1
Volume Twenty	£6.99	978-1-84161 304-8

Gift Books		
30 Years - The Fun's Just Begun	£9.99	978-1-84161-307-9
Don't Know, Don't Care	£4.99	978-1-84161-279-9
Get a Grip	£4.99	978-1-84161-282-9
I Don't Do Ordinary	£4.99	978-1-84161-281-2
Keep your Attitude, I have my own	£4.99	978-1-84161-278-2

Little Books		
C-c-c-caffeine	£2.50	978-1-84161-183-9
Food 'n' Fitness	£2.50	978-1-84161-145-7
Laughs	£2.50	978-1-84161-146-4
Love 'n' Stuff	£2.50	978-1-84161-147-1
Surf 'n' Sun	£2.50	978-1-84161-186-0
The Office	£2.50	978-1-84161-184-6
Zzzzzz	£2.50	978-1-84161-185-3

Miscellaneous		
Colour Collection Book 3 (Aug 09)	£11.99	978-1-84161-320-8
Colour Collection Book 2	£10.99	978-1-84161-306-2
Colour Collection Book 1	£10.99	978-1-84161-293-5
Treasury 7	£10.99	978-1-84161-248-5
Treasury 6	£10.99	978-1-84161-229-4
Treasury 5	£10.99	978-1-84161-198-3
Treasury 4	£10.99	978-1-84161-180-8
Treasury 3	£9.99	978-1-84161-142-6

All Garfield books are available at your local bookshop or from the publisher at the address below.

Just send your order with your payment and name and address details to:-

Ravette Publishing Ltd, PO Box 876, Horsham,
West Sussex RH12 9GH
(tel: 01403 711443 ... email: ingrid@ravettepub.co.uk

Prices and availability are subject to change without notice.

Please enclose a cheque or postal order made payable to **Ravette Publishing** to the value of the cover price of the book/s and allow the following for UK postage and packing:-

70p for the first book + 40p for each additional book
except Treasuries & Colour Collections... when please add £3.00 per copy